WHEN YOU
DON'T KNOW
WHAT *to Say*

WHEN YOU
DON'T KNOW
WHAT *to Say*

WORDS *of* CARING *for* ALL OCCASIONS

Discovery House Publishers

Books, music, and videos that feed the soul with the Word of God

Box 3566 Grand Rapids, MI 49501

Discovery House Publishers is affiliated with RBC Ministries, Grand Rapids, Michigan.

Discovery House books are distributed to the trade exclusively by Barbour Publishing, Inc., Uhrichsville, Ohio.

Scripture quotations are from the New International Version (NIV) © 1973, 1978, 1984 by International Bible Society and are used by permission of Zondervan Bible Publishers. All rights reserved.

Design and typesetting by Lakeside Design Plus

Printed in the United States of America

07 08 09 10 / BP / 10 9 8 7 6 5 4 3 2 1

$\mathcal{C}$ONTENTS

GETTING STARTED

There was a time when the written word was the only means of communicating with people over long distance. Modern innovations like text messaging, e-mails, and cell phones have made communication easier and faster, but, as a result, handwritten messages have become a rare treasure. When someone actually takes the time to send a note or write a letter, it becomes more meaningful, more personal, and more permanent. It becomes a record of thoughts and sentiments that can be revisited and cherished time and again.

We want to help you show your family, friends, acquaintances, and others who may cross your path how much you care by taking the time to write. To feed the soul of a friend or loved one who may be celebrating one of life's joyous events or struggling through a time of difficulty.

Proverbs 25:11 tells us that "a word spoken in right circumstances" is "like apples of gold in settings of silver." Yet many people struggle with finding "just the right words" to say "in right circumstances." So we want to help you get started by providing you with some appropriate sentiments and Scriptures in this book. We've also included some of our favorite devotional thoughts from some of our favorite authors.

Whether you want to wish your neighbor a happy birthday or offer a message of support to that person at church who is struggling with the loss of a loved one, the process is as easy as looking through this volume and finding the right category. When you do, you will find a variety of messages. Choose the one that suits your situation best, and use it to bless another person with the right words. Mix and match sentiments and Scriptures as you think appropriate. Or use the sentiments here as a springboard to create your own message—sometimes just the right prompt can get your own creative juices flowing!

However you choose to use these "right words," we are sure that those who receive them will be encouraged to know that you have cared enough to take the time to write.

Genuine Love

We can easily describe what it feels like to "be loved," but we have trouble translating that into what it means to "be loving." We feel loved when someone wants to be with us, takes the risk of letting us know him, takes the time to get to know us, and always does what is in our best interest. Our desire to be on the receiving end of this kind of devotion is much greater than our ability to return it.

To be loved is one of the strongest of all desires. The need for love is as much a part of God's design for humans as the need for air, water, and food. We can't lead a healthy life without it . . . One of the ways God passes along His love is through others, generally those closest to us. . . .

The Bible describes love in this familiar New Testament passage:

> Love is patient, love is kind. It does not envy, it does not boast, it is not proud. It is not rude, it is not self-seeking, it is not easily angered, it keeps no record of wrongs. Love does not delight in evil but rejoices with the truth. It always protects, always trusts, always hopes, always perseveres.
>
> —1 Corinthians 13:4–7

In other words, love seeks the highest good. God's love is perfect because He seeks the highest good for all creation. Every human being longs to be the recipient of this kind of love, but no human can provide it. The only place to experience genuine love is in a relationship with the One whose very being defines it. Not only is God the perfect example of love, He *is* love, and apart from His love for us none of us could love or be loved.

> We love because he first loved us.
>
> —1 John 4:19

—Julie Ackerman Link
The Art of Loving God

what to say

BIRTHDAY

Today is a day to celebrate YOU!

Have a happy day
and a year full of wishes
come true.

Happy Birthday

I thank my God
every time I remember you.
In all my prayers for . . . you,
I always pray with joy.

PHILIPPIANS 1 : 3 – 4

To a wonderful friend
   on your birthday—
Sending lots of wishes that your
   day will be filled
   with delightful moments,
And your year will overflow
   with God's blessings.

Happy Birthday

Teach us to number our days aright,
that we may gain a heart of wisdom.

A Birthday Blessing

God's grace be with you,
His peace surround you,
His love enfold you
On your birthday and always.

Happy Birthday

*Grace to you and peace
from God our Father and
the Lord Jesus Christ.*

PHILEMON 3

Wishing you a birthday
that is filled with all things
you count as special:
Good friends,
Dear family,
And joy to last all year.

*The joy of the Lord
is your strength.*

NEHEMIAH 8:10

what to say

GRADUATION

Graduation brings pride and joy
    for past accomplishments
    and excitement for the future
        that lies ahead.

Congratulations
    on your graduation.

*"For I know the plans
I have for you," declares the Lord,
    "plans to prosper you
    and not to harm you,
plans to give you hope and a future."*

JEREMIAH 29:11

On your graduation,
may God richly bless you
in all you do.

May he give you
the desire of your heart
and make all your plans succeed.

PSALM 20:4

As you graduate
    and face whatever life may bring,
    may God's hand guide
        your every step.

In his heart a man plans his course,
but the Lord determines his steps.

PROVERBS 16:9

Congratulations
on your graduation!

Great challenges lie ahead.
Great opportunities
are before you.
Go in God's grace and love
as your future unfolds.

*I can do everything
through him who gives me strength.*

PHILIPPIANS 4:13

Congratulations
on your graduation!

Whatever your future holds,
Wherever your life takes you,
God's gracious hand
will guide you.
His love will surround you.

*Be strong and courageous . . .
for the Lord your God
will be with you wherever you go.*

JOSHUA 1:9

Looking for Comfort

I often quote Psalm 27 to encourage people who are going through a difficult time. The psalmist was living in very unpleasant circumstances, yet he expected to "see the goodness of the Lord in the land of the living" (v. 13). But I now have many friends who are ill or bedridden with no prospect of getting better. How can they find comfort in these words?

We could emphasize the truth that our ultimate hope resides not in this present life but in the world now unseen, our future home in heaven (2 Corinthians 4:18; 5:1–8). Even though that is true, it seems that the psalmist was speaking of an expectation in this present world, "in the land of the living," rather than the next world.

So let's look more closely at the psalmist's hope. His expectation was not necessarily deliverance from bad circumstances but the hope of seeing "the goodness of the Lord." That's something we can see even in times of trouble.

When my friend Maurice was hospitalized due to a stroke from which he was told he would never totally recover, he said to me, "While flat on my back, I have been thinking about God. I sense His goodness and greatness as never before."

No matter what your situation, you can find evidence of God's goodness—so keep looking for it with hope.

—Herb Vander Lugt
Our Daily Bread

what to say

COMFORT

May the Father of compassion
and the God of all comfort
surround you with love.

Praise be to the God and Father
of our Lord Jesus Christ,
the Father of compassion and
the God of all comfort,
who comforts us in all our troubles.

2 CORINTHIANS 1:3–4

To comfort you—
   May good friends surround you,
   God's love enfold you,
   and the Spirit's presence
      bring you peace.

You will keep in perfect peace
him whose mind is steadfast,
   because he trusts in you.

ISAIAH 26:3

34

In our time of need
 the Spirit surrounds us
 with His love
 and fills our hearts with peace.

Cast your cares on the Lord
and he will sustain you;
he will never let the righteous fall.

PSALM 55:22

In this difficult time
  may the peace of the Spirit
    fill your heart,
  the love of the Father
    renew your strength,
  and the promise of the Savior
    bring you hope.

*Jesus said, "I have told you these
things, so that in me you may
have peace. In this world you will
have trouble. But take heart!
I have overcome the world."*

JOHN 16:33

36

The God of all comfort
    supplies us with—
        strength to face today,
        hope to face tomorrow,
        and peace to face the future.

*The Lord gives strength
to his people; the Lord blesses
his people with peace.*

PSALM 29:11

May the love of Christ
   comfort you in this difficult time
   and bring you peace.

*I will never leave you
   nor forsake you.*

JOSHUA 1:5

Through the darkest hours,
the longest nights,
the loneliest moment,
God's love will surround you,
His strength will uphold you,
His peace will fill your heart.

*He gives strength to the weary and
increases the power of the weak.*

ISAIAH 40:29

Comfort comes in many ways—
a thoughtful prayer,
a gentle smile,
a loving hug.

*Be kind and compassionate
to one another.*

EPHESIANS 4:32

God has promised:
   Though grief may
   overshadow you,
      it will not consume you.
   Though sorrow fills your soul,
      it will fade away.
   Our deepest sympathy.

This I call to mind and
therefore I have hope:
Because of the Lord's great love
we are not consumed,
for his compassions never fail.
They are new every morning;
great is your faithfulness.

LAMENTATIONS 3:21–23

Although your world is shaken,
God stands firm and
holds you fast
in His loving arms.

The eternal God is your refuge, and
underneath are the everlasting arms.

DEUTERONOMY 33:27

what to say . . .

FRIENDSHIP

I took a moment today
to think of you
and thank God for your
enduring friendship.
Thank you for being
such a great friend.

A friend loves at all times.

PROVERBS 17:17

Just wanted to let you know
I've been blessed . . .
With thoughts of you
and our friendship.

*A happy heart
makes the face cheerful.*

PROVERBS 15:13

Through gales of laughter,
Through tears of sorrow,
Through times I couldn't face alone,
You were there for me.
Thank you so very much.
Your friendship
means everything to me.

*I thank my God
every time I remember you.*

PHILIPPIANS 1 : 3

Good friends stand with you
    on the mountaintop and applaud.

Best friends walk with you
    through the valley
    and hold your hand.

Thanks for being my best friend.

Two are better than one . . .
        If one falls down,
    his friend can help him up.

ECCLESIASTES 4:9–10

Having you for a friend
has added an abundance
of joy to my life.

What a blessing you are.

Dear children, let us not love
with words or tongue
but with actions and in truth.

1 JOHN 3:18

The Rx for Laughter

"A cheerful heart is good medicine"

—Proverbs 17:22

I t's been rough," my friend said, "but I've finally made it through!" We were celebrating the completion of a miserable, but necessary, year of chemotherapy in her battle against cancer.

She leaned back and looked at me thoughtfully. "You'll never know how much I appreciated all those cards, notes, and letters you sent to me day after day."

I laughed and told her that she *should* appreciate them since I'm usually the world's most inconsistent letter-writer. But I explained that God had assigned me "mailbox duty" that year. And along with the assignment He gave me an unusual sense of eagerness and joy about it, so if the letters had helped she should thank *Him*.

"Well, the love and encouragement kept me going," she said. "But do you know what I appreciated more than anything else in those letters? Those funny, silly things you wrote that made me *laugh*. Because at a time like that, just when it's most needed, laughter is the hardest to find."

Truly, laughter is a gift that we can give to one another—a gift meant to be shared. Laughter, joy, and just plain fun have a way of building strength into friendships. Laughter creates memories. It is life's bubbles and often its best medicine. And strips of shining laughter weave friendship's basket tight enough to hold the tears.

> A happy heart makes the face cheerful, but heartache crushes the spirit . . . All the days of the oppressed are wretched, but the cheerful heart has a continual feast . . . A cheerful look brings joy to the heart, and good news gives health to the bones.
>
> —Proverbs 15:13, 15, 30

> However many years a man [woman] may live, let him [her] enjoy them all. But let him [her] remember the days of darkness, for they will be many.
>
> —Ecclesiastes 11:8

> I know that there is nothing better for men [women] than to be happy and do good while they live.
>
> —Ecclesiastes 3:12

—Susan Lenzkes
Crossing the Bridge Between You and Me

what to say...

GET WELL

While you get well . . .
   May God's love bring you comfort,
   His promises bring you peace,
   His faithfulness bring you hope.

The Lord will sustain him
on his sickbed
and restore him
from his bed of illness.

PSALM 41:3

This little note
  brings words of cheer
  and my hope that you are better
  soon.

And the God of all grace . . .
  will himself restore you
  and make you strong.

1 PETER 5:10

A prayer for your recovery:
    May God's arms enfold you,
    His peace surround you,
    His loving hands heal you.

I am the Lord, your God,
who takes hold of your right hand
and says to you, Do not fear;
I will help you.

ISAIAH 41:13

As you wait to get well,
  Be patient.
  God is working day by day
  to restore your strength,
  renew your spirit
  and return you to complete health.

Those who hope in the Lord
  will renew their strength.
  They will soar
  on wings like eagles;
they will run and not grow weary,
they will walk and not be faint.

ISAIAH 40:31

We do not know why we are asked
    to endure pain and sickness.
What we do know is that God
will stand by our side
    and see us through.
May you feel God's presence as
He brings you back to health.

The Lord is faithful to all his promises
and loving toward all he has made.

PSALM 145:13

Just wanted to let you know—
   I'm hoping
   you get stronger each day
   and are soon feeling better.

Get well soon.

Be strong and take heart,
all you who hope in the Lord.

PSALM 31:24

what to say

THINKING
OF YOU

Thinking of you and praying
that God's blessings
will be showered upon you
throughout your day.

*My God will meet all your needs
according to his glorious riches
in Christ Jesus.*

PHILIPPIANS 4:19

My mind is filled
with happy thoughts—
all of you.
Just wanted to let you know
you brought a smile to my day.

*I thank my God
every time I remember you.*

PHILIPPIANS 1:3

Thinking of you
and praying you will be renewed
by God's presence.

*He gives strength to the weary
and increases the power of the weak.*

Isaiah 40:29

Thinking of you
and praying God's peace
will fill your heart and mind.

You [O Lord]
will keep in perfect peace
him whose mind is steadfast,
because he trusts in you.

ISAIAH 26:3

Just wanted to say—
   I'm hoping
      this little note of cheer
  brings a smile to your face
     and laughter to your life.

May the God of hope fill you
with all joy and peace
as you trust in him.

ROMANS 15:13

Just wanted you to know . . .
   I thought of you today
   And it filled my day with joy.

I have not stopped
giving thanks for you,
remembering you in my prayers.

EPHESIANS 1:16

Remembering What God Has Done

Throughout Scripture God emphasizes the importance of remembering, and He encourages the use of memory devices. One of the first examples is found in the first book of the Bible. God placed a rainbow in the sky to remind Himself of His promise to never again destroy all life with a flood (Genesis 9:13–16).

Many years later when Moses addressed six hundred thousand recently freed slaves and their families, he told the people to use memory devices to help them remember the commandments God had given to them.

> Tie them as symbols on your hands and bind them on your foreheads. Write them on the doorframes of your houses and on your gates.
>
> —Deuteronomy 6:8–9

God told the Israelites to remember such things as: the Sabbath (Exodus 20:8); the things you have seen (i.e., what God has done) (Deuteronomy 4:9); that God brought them out of slavery (Deuteronomy 5:15); the Lord, His laws, His decrees (Deuteronomy 8:11); that God is God and there is no other (Isaiah 46:9).

To help people remember, God established an assortment of holiday celebrations during which the people were to stop working and take time to remember and enjoy everything God had done for them (see Leviticus 23).

All religious holidays are in fact memory devices. Christians have a set of holidays to remember the life and work of Christ.

—Julie Ackerman Link
Loving God with All My Mind

what to say

THANKSGIVING

Happy Thanksgiving

With grateful hearts
   we gather together
and give thanks to God
   for our bounty of blessings.
Wishing you and your loved ones
   a blessed Thanksgiving.

Give thanks to the Lord,
   for he is good;
His love endures forever.

PSALM 118:1

Thinking of you at Thanksgiving

At Thanksgiving I thank God
for all He has given me—
especially for friends like you.

Have a blessed Thanksgiving,
my friend.

Enter his gates with thanksgiving
and his courts with praise;
give thanks to him
and praise his name.
For the Lord is good
and his love endures forever.

PSALM 100:4

78

With grateful hearts
   we give thanks to God
   for family and friends,
   for home and health
      and happiness.

Have a blessed Thanksgiving Day.

You are my God,
and I will give you thanks;
you are my God,
and I will exalt you.

PSALM 118:28

On this day of thanksgiving,
   We remember God's blessings
      and give Him thanks:
For our home, our health,
   our family, our friends,
   our freedom.

Have a wonderful
   Thanksgiving Day.

How great you are,
O Sovereign Lord!
There is no one like you,
and there is no God but you.

2 SAMUEL 7:22

what to say

CHRISTMAS

Into a world of darkness He came . . .
  The Prince of Peace
  The King of Glory
  The Hope of the World

Let us rejoice!

For God so loved the world
that he gave his one and only Son,
that whoever believes in him
shall not perish but have eternal life.

JOHN 3:16

Just as the angels sang
   to announce Christ's birth,
   Let us sing the songs
      of Christmas
   and tell the world of God's love.

Merry Christmas.

Sing and make music
in your heart to the Lord.

EPHESIANS 5:19

With joy we welcome
the coming of Christ
and celebrate
this holy time of year.
May you have
a blessed Christmas season.

For to us a child is born,
to us a son is given.

ISAIAH 9:6

Be joyful and sing.
    Christ has come
        to bring joy to the world.

Have a blessed Christmas
    and a joyous New Year.

Light has come into the world.

JOHN 3:19

Music fills the world
   with the songs of Christmas.

Rejoice and sing—
   our Savior is born!

*Today in the town of David
a Savior has been born to you;
   he is Christ the Lord.*

LUKE 2:11

Merry Christmas

May Christmas bring you
blessings of family and friends.

May your New Year be filled
with God's goodness.

The Lord has done great things for us,
and we are filled with joy.

PSALM 126:3

what to say

EASTER

89

This Easter,
  may you know Mary's thrill
  at hearing the words:

  "He is not here. He is risen!"

Happy Easter

The angel said . . . "He is not here;
he has risen, just as he said."

MATTHEW 28 : 5 – 6

At Easter and always
  may the announcement
    "He Lives"
  fill your heart with joy.

Praise be to the God and Father
  of our Lord Jesus Christ!
    In his great mercy
  he has given us new birth
    into a living hope
  through the resurrection
of Jesus Christ from the dead.

1 PETER 1 : 3

Christ lives . . .
   To rule over our lives
   And reign supreme
      in our world.

Thanks be to God!
He gives us the victory
through our Lord Jesus Christ.

1 CORINTHIANS 15:57

Christ is risen! Hallelujah!
  Christ's resurrection
  floods our lives
    with hope and joy.
  Have a blessed Easter.

Christ Jesus . . . has destroyed death
and has brought life
and immortality to light
through the gospel.

2 TIMOTHY 1:10

94

Caught Off Balance

"For I am the Lord your God, who takes hold
of your right hand and says to you, Do not fear;
I will help you."

—Isaiah 41:13

Sudden loss, besides leaving us hurt and be-
wildered, can leave us listing seriously to
one side. This state of imbalance is surprising, if

not downright frightening. We had no idea we were leaning so heavily on a person, job, or ability until it was yanked away without warning.

When a loved one who partially defines who we are (or who we are *not*) is taken away by death, distance, divorce, or disagreement, our grief is intensified by the loss of this part of ourselves. Maybe we had depended on the person to express emotion for us or to think or decide for us. Perhaps the person was our sense of humor, our planner, our conscience, our practical side, our memory, or even our proof of worth. In one way or another, that person was our *balance*. And now we are *off* balance.

It is not just the loss of a person that can throw us off balance. Sometimes the loss of a job, ability, ideal, attribute, or goal carries with it a large chunk of our self-esteem, identity, or purpose, leaving us feeling lopsided and ready to topple over. When this happens, it may be time to confess that our sense of well-being was improperly anchored. We may also discover that our vision needs to expand—that who we are is more than what we do or how we look, and that the sum of our worth is far more than any loss.

God's secure love and His sure promise to care for us are the perfect ballast; they provide stability without adding weight to our load. When our lives are filled with Jesus Christ and the security, worth, and identity He provides, the losses we experience cannot destabilize us.

We may still toss and turn in stormy weather, but we'll never run aground or be shipwrecked.

Find rest, O my soul, in God alone; my hope comes from him. He alone is my rock and my salvation; he is my fortress, I will not be shaken. My salvation and my honor depend on God; he is my mighty rock, my refuge. Trust in him at all times, O people; pour out your hearts to him, for God is our refuge.

—Psalm 62:5–8

I waited patiently for the Lord; he turned to me and heard my cry. He lifted me out of the slimy pit, out of the mud and mire; he set my feet on a rock and gave me a firm place to stand. He put a new song in my mouth, a hymn of praise to our God. Many will see and fear and put their trust in the Lord. Blessed is the man who makes the Lord his trust, who does not look to the proud, to those who turn aside to false gods.

—Psalm 40:1–4

—Susan Lenzkes
When Life Takes What Matters

what to say . . .

SYMPATHY

You are in my thoughts and
   prayers as you grieve your loss.

God bless you and keep you close
   in your time of sadness.

For I am the Lord, your God,
who takes hold of your right hand
and says to you, Do not fear;
I will help you.

ISAIAH 41:13

Through your tears
and in your sorrow,
know that God holds you close.

Be still and know that I am God.

PSALM 46:10

Tears will come
   and grief may consume us,
     but we have hope.

The day is coming
   when death's pain
     will be no more.

He will swallow up death forever.
The Sovereign Lord
will wipe away the tears
from all faces.

ISAIAH 25:8

Faith is our comfort as we grieve.
　May your faith
　　in Christ's promises
　　bring you peace.

You will keep in perfect peace
him whose mind is steadfast,
because he trusts in you.

ISAIAH 26:3

Comfort comes in knowing
death is not the end.

Those who die in Christ
will live eternally.

Death has been swallowed up in
victory. Thanks be to God!
He gives us the victory
through our Lord Jesus Christ.

1 CORINTHIANS 15:54, 57

May the memories of your loved one . . .
  of happy times,
  of joyful smiles,
  of hearty laughter,
  and caring words

Help you through this sorrowful time.

Whatever is true,
whatever is noble, whatever is right,
whatever is pure, whatever is lovely,
whatever is admirable—
if anything is excellent or praiseworthy—
think about such things.

PHILIPPIANS 4 : 8

As you grieve.

God has promised
 that comfort will come,
 that peace will be restored,
 that tears will eventually cease.

He will wipe every tear from their eyes.
There will be no more death
or mourning or crying or pain,
for the old order of things
has passed away.

REVELATION 21:4

Your loved one was a joy to know
and a shining example
of Christ's love.

My deepest sympathy
for your great loss.

In my Father's house
are many rooms; if it were not so,
I would have told you.
I am going there to prepare
a place for you.

JOHN 14:2

God's ways
    are sometimes mysterious.
    We do not understand
        this pain and loss,
    but we trust and have faith
        that God's way is perfect.
    With deepest sympathy.

In all things
God works for the good
of those who love him.

ROMANS 8:28

Your pain and sorrow are shared
by family and friends.

May you find comfort
in knowing so many care.

My thoughts and prayers
are with you.

Blessed are those who mourn,
for they will be comforted.

MATTHEW 5 : 4

what to say

Thank You

Thank you for your kindness.
You have shown me God's love.

God is love. Whoever lives in love
lives in God, and God in him.

1 JOHN 4:16

God has showered me
  with blessings through you.

Thank you for all you've done
  to help me through
  this difficult time.

Let us encourage one another.

Hebrews 10:25

Your thoughtfulness
  means so much to me.

Thank you for your kind words,
  your caring actions,
  your constant prayers.

He who does what is right
is righteous, just as he is righteous.

1 J O H N 3 : 7

I thank God every day
that He has sent you
into my life.

Thank you for your thoughtfulness
and caring.

Dear friends,
let us love one another,
for love comes from God.
Everyone who loves
has been born of God and knows God.

1 JOHN 4:7

"Thank you" is such a small phrase
to express my feelings
for all you've done.

Your willingness to help
was greatly appreciated.

*As we have opportunity,
let us do good to all people.*

GALATIANS 6:10

Worth the Risk

If we build more windows and fewer walls we
will have more friends.

—Alan Loy McGinnis, *The Friendship Factor*

When we trust another person enough
to tell her who we really are and
how we really feel, we have shared our most
precious possession. But for many of us, such
openness seems like the ultimate risk. We feel

vulnerable. What if we are taken lightly, belit-tled, betrayed, rudely corrected, abandoned, or rejected? Painful experiences flash their warning lights within us: *Danger! Do not enter!*

Such fears can give us a healthy sense of cau-tion about indiscriminately stripping bare our soul to total strangers, or to people who have not shown themselves to be trustworthy. From such experiences we can learn the wisdom of a gradual process of discovery and disclosure.

But caution has gone beyond discretion when it keeps us closed off from others, living in fear of revealing who, what, and where we are. For not only is it healthy, right, and good to know and be known as we go through life, but there will inevitably come a time when we desper-ately need the ministry of someone who already understands and loves us.

One day I was sitting on the floor, working on a project with a friend. She seemed unusually quiet and withdrawn. Sensing trouble and not wanting my friend to suffer an internal explo-sion that could do serious damage when there would be no one around to administer first aid, I began to probe gently. At my subtle inquiries, she dodged and slid sideways, so I let it go and we continued our work.

During a break, I leaned against the wall, drew my legs to my chest, rested my chin on my knees, and began to share an area of need that could have made me vulnerable to her judgment. She listened with empathy, expressed her support, and finally said, "You shared that with me so that I'd be able to talk about what's wrong, didn't you?"

"Who, *me*?" I laughed, and then grew serious as her pain tumbled out in a heartrending torrent.

Later her world fell apart, and I will never forget what she said: "I'm so glad I shared with you before. I don't have to explain anything now. You already know. You see, I *couldn't* explain anything now. I'd have been *alone* in this. . . ."

Through openness, we had built a bridge of friendship that she could run across in a crisis—run to understanding, comfort, caring, and help. An emergency is not time to start a building project.

Keep on living an open, transparent life, because that is where the Spirit blooms and produces fruit in authentic relationships and demonstrates the kind of life God approves.

As we continue to share honestly with each other, we help one another grow to our full potential as Christians in unity with Christ our head. As each of us stays in union and harmony with Christ, we are energized and consequently give energy to others through Christ, enabling them in their growth and giving love to the family as a whole.

Discover new ways of expressing your new, unique personhood in Christ, ways which are in harmony with who you really are . . . This new behavior will demonstrate that you have a right relationship with yourself and with God and are becoming a whole person. Stop playing games, and be straight in your communication, because we are all dependent on each other.
—Ephesians 5:8–10; 4:15–16, 24–25 (from *The Heart of Paul: A Relational Paraphrase of the New Testament* by Ben Campbell Johnson)

—Susan Lenzkes
Crossing the Bridge Between You and Me

what to say ...

WEDDING

In your new life together,
may your sorrows be few
and your joys be as abundant
as the sands of the seashore.

Satisfy us in the morning
with your unfailing love,
that we may sing for joy
and be glad all our days.

PSALM 90:14

Your marriage—
  two lives
  united in Christ
  and surrounded by God's love.

The Lord bless you and keep you;
The Lord make his face shine
upon you and be gracious to you;
The Lord turn his face toward you
and give you peace.

NUMBERS 6:24–26

May the hopes and dreams
   you hold in your hearts today
be fulfilled in
   your lifetime together.

Commit to the Lord
whatever you do,
and your plans will succeed.

PROVERBS 16:3

May God's love surround you,
His peace enfold you,
His faithfulness guard you
throughout your life together.

Live a life of love,
just as Christ loved us.

EPHESIANS 5:2

May your love deepen
through the years

And your joys multiply
in your life together.

[Love] always protects,
always trusts, always hopes,
always perseveres.
Love never fails.

1 CORINTHIANS 13:7–8

what to say

Anniversary

A marriage with God at its center
   will last a lifetime.

Congratulations on your
   exemplary life together.

*For this God is our God for ever
and ever; he will be our guide
even to the end.*

P SALM 4 8 : 1 4

Happy Anniversary.

It's a day to remember
the love you've shared

And to rejoice in the joy
you've known throughout
the years!

Congratulations!

Now these three remain:
faith, hope and love.
But the greatest of these is love.

1 CORINTHIANS 13:13

Though the memories and
photos of your wedding day
may fade with time,

Your love for one another
continues to shine brightly
with each new day.

Congratulations on
your wedding anniversary.

*[Love] always protects,
always trusts, always hopes,
always perseveres.*

1 CORINTHIANS 13:7

Today is the day to celebrate
 the love you share as a couple

And the joy your life together
 has brought to so many others.

Happy Anniversary!

Live a life of love,
just as Christ loved us.

EPHESIANS 5:2

Your anniversary is the perfect day
to celebrate your life of love.

Congratulations!

He who pursues righteousness and
love finds life, prosperity
and honor.

P R O V E R B S   2 1 : 2 1

what to say

NEW BABY

One small new life—

But oh, what surprises will unfold
   in the years to come!

*Every good and perfect gift
is from above.*

JAMES 1:17

Made in God's image
  Born in His love

A baby—God's wonder,
  His gift from above.

*In the image of God
has God made man.*

GENESIS 9:6

Gazing into a newborn's eyes,
one sees the face of God.

The Lord bless you and keep you;
The Lord make his face shine
upon you and be gracious to you;
The Lord turn his face toward you
and give you peace.

Numbers 6:24–26

A new baby reminds us
   of what wonderful gifts
     God sends us.
Congratulations
   on your new little one.

I praise you because
I am fearfully and wonderfully made;
your works are wonderful,
I know that full well.

PSALM 139:14

Addresses and Special Dates

Name: _____

Address: _____

_____

Anniversary: _____ Birthday: _____

Additional Information: _____

_____

_____

Name: _____

Address: _____

_____

Anniversary: _____ Birthday: _____

Additional Information: _____

_____

_____

Name: _____

Address: _____

_____

Anniversary: _____ Birthday: _____

Additional Information: _____

_____

_____

Name: _____

Address: _____

_____

Anniversary: _____ Birthday: _____

Additional Information: _____

_____

_____

Name: _____

Address: _____

_____

Anniversary: _____ Birthday: _____

Additional Information: _____

_____

_____

Name: _____

Address: _____

_____

Anniversary: _____ Birthday: _____

Additional Information: _____

_____

_____

Name: _____

Address: _____

_____

Anniversary: _____ Birthday: _____

Additional Information: _____

_____

_____

Name: _____

Address: _____

_____

Anniversary: _____ Birthday: _____

Additional Information: _____

_____

_____

Name: _____

Address: _____

_____

Anniversary: _____ Birthday: _____

Additional Information: _____

_____

_____

Name: _____

Address: _____

_____

Anniversary: _____ Birthday: _____

Additional Information: _____

_____

_____

Name: _____

Address: _____

_____

Anniversary: _____ Birthday: _____

Additional Information: _____

_____

_____

Name: _____

Address: _____

_____

Anniversary: _____ Birthday: _____

Additional Information: _____

_____

_____

Name: _____

Address: _____

_____

Anniversary: _____ Birthday: _____

Additional Information: _____

_____

_____

Name: _____

Address: _____

_____

Anniversary: _____ Birthday: _____

Additional Information: _____

_____

_____

Name: _____

Address: _____

_____

Anniversary: _____ Birthday: _____

Additional Information: _____

_____

_____

Name: _____

Address: _____

_____

Anniversary: _____ Birthday: _____

Additional Information: _____

_____

_____

Name: _____

Address: _____

_____

Anniversary: _____ Birthday: _____

Additional Information: _____

_____

_____

Name: _____

Address: _____

_____

Anniversary: _____ Birthday: _____

Additional Information: _____

_____

_____

Name: _____

Address: _____

_____

Anniversary: _____ Birthday: _____

Additional Information: _____

_____

_____

Name: _____

Address: _____

_____

Anniversary: _____ Birthday: _____

Additional Information: _____

_____

_____

Name: _____

Address: _____

_____

Anniversary: _____ Birthday: _____

Additional Information: _____

_____

_____

Name: _____

Address: _____

_____

Anniversary: _____ Birthday: _____

Additional Information: _____

_____

_____

Name: _____

Address: _____

_____

Anniversary: _____ Birthday: _____

Additional Information: _____

_____

_____

Name: _____

Address: _____

_____

Anniversary: _____ Birthday: _____

Additional Information: _____

_____

_____

Name: _____

Address: _____

_____

Anniversary: _____ Birthday: _____

Additional Information: _____

_____

_____

Name: _____

Address: _____

_____

Anniversary: _____ Birthday: _____

Additional Information: _____

_____

_____

Name: _____

Address: _____

_____

Anniversary: _____ Birthday: _____

Additional Information: _____

_____

_____

Name: _____

Address: _____

_____

Anniversary: _____ Birthday: _____

Additional Information: _____

_____

_____

Name: _____

Address: _____

_____

Anniversary: _____ Birthday: _____

Additional Information: _____

_____

_____

Name: _____

Address: _____

_____

Anniversary: _____ Birthday: _____

Additional Information: _____

_____

_____

Name: _____

Address: _____

_____

Anniversary: _____ Birthday: _____

Additional Information: _____

_____

_____

Name: _____

Address: _____

_____

Anniversary: _____ Birthday: _____

Additional Information: _____

_____

_____

Name: _____

Address: _____

_____

Anniversary: _____ Birthday: _____

Additional Information: _____

_____

_____

Name: _____

Address: _____

_____

Anniversary: _____ Birthday: _____

Additional Information: _____

_____

_____

Name: _____

Address: _____

_____

Anniversary: _____ Birthday: _____

Additional Information: _____

_____

_____

Name: _____

Address: _____

_____

Anniversary: _____ Birthday: _____

Additional Information: _____

_____

_____

Name: _____

Address: _____

_____

Anniversary: _____ Birthday: _____

Additional Information: _____

_____

_____

Name: _____

Address: _____

_____

Anniversary: _____ Birthday: _____

Additional Information: _____

_____

_____

Name: _____

Address: _____

_____

Anniversary: _____ Birthday: _____

Additional Information: _____

_____

_____

Note to the Reader

The publisher invites you to share your response to the message of this book by writing Discovery House Publishers, P.O. Box 3566, Grand Rapids, MI 49501, U.S.A. For information about other Discovery House books, music, videos, or DVDs, contact us at the same address or call 1-800-653-8333. Find us on the Internet at http://www.dhp.org/ or send e-mail to books@dhp.org.